Greetings From
Hawaii

Greetings From
Hawaii

Greetings From
Hawaii

Greetings from
Hawaii

Hawaii

Greetings From
Hawaii

Greetings from
Hawaii

74
72
Greetings From
Hawaii

Greetings from
Hawaii

74
72
Greetings from
Hawaii

74
72
Greetings From
Hawaii

74
72
Greetings from
Hawaii

74°
72°
Greetings from
Hawaii

Hawaii

Greetings from
Hawaii

Greetings from
Hawaii

74°
72
Greetings From
Hawaii

Greetings From
Hawaii

Greetings From
Hawaii

74
72
Hawaii

74
72
Greetings from
Hawaii

Hawaii

74
72
Greetings From
Hawaii

74°
72
Greetings from
Hawaii

Hawaii

Hawaii

Greetings From
Hawaii

Greetings From
Hawaii

Greetings From
Hawaii

Greetings from
Hawaii

Greetings From
Hawaii

74°
72
Hawaii

Greetings from
Hawaii

Hawaii

74
72
Hawaii

Greetings from
Hawaii

74
72
Greetings from
Hawaii

74°
72
Greetings From
Hawaii

Greetings From
Hawaii

74
72
Greetings From
Hawaii

74°
72
Hawaii

79
72
Hawaii

Greetings from
Hawaii

74
72
Hawaii

Greetings From
Hawaii

Greetings From
Hawaii

Hawaii

Greetings From
Hawaii

Greetings From
Hawaii

Hawaii

Greetings from
Hawaii

74
72
Greetings from
Hawaii

Greetings From
Hawaii

Hawaii

Greetings From
Hawaii

Greetings from
Hawaii

74°
72
Hawaii

Greetings from
Hawaii

74
72
Greetings From
Hawaii

Greetings from
Hawaii

Greetings From
Hawaii

74°
72
Greetings From
Hawaii

Greetings from
Hawaii

Greetings From
Hawaii

Greetings from
Hawaii

Greetings From
Hawaii

Greetings From
Hawaii

Greetings From
Hawaii

Greetings from
Hawaii

Greetings From
Hawaii

Hawaii

Hawaii

Greetings From
Hawaii

74
72
Greetings From
Hawaii

Greetings from
Hawaii

Printed in the USA
CPSIA information can be obtained
at www.ICGtesting.com
CBHW030125220624
10446CB00042B/513

9 798385 412730